T2-AKX-913

The Wonders of
MOTHER'S MILK

by Mishawn Purnell-O'Neal

art by Dana T.C. Simpson

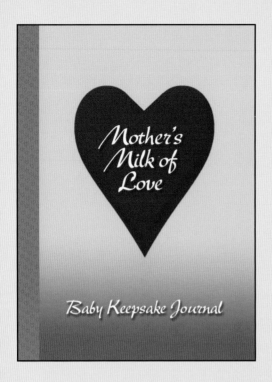

Also available from author
Mishawn Purnell-O'Neal

**Mother's Milk of Love:
Baby Keepsake Journal**

A delightful baby journal that weaves
baby's precious memories in a story-
book of love told straight from the
heart of the mother.

Hardcover/Spiral Bound
28 pages
ISBN: #0-9712199-1-5
$21.00

To order:
www.breast-feedingamerica.com

The Wonders of Mother's Milk

To order:
www.breast-feedingamerica.com

To the men in my life —
my husband Marcus and
my son's Makail and Micah.
You are my inspiration
and the reason I am able
to do what I do.
—MPO

Mothers milk is like no other.

Every day new wonders are being told.

With all the good things known about mother's milk

some even ask, "Is it more precious than gold?"

A mother who gives her baby her milk
does so with love and a smile.
Because she knows that she is providing the
healthiest start to her growing child.

Mother's milk is unique.
It provides food and health protection.
From within each and every drop
good things come bursting from all directions.

Since the beginning of time
mothers have been feeding their babies in this way.
In many places around the world
it is the only food that some babies receive all day.

For years mother's milk
has been used for many different things.
Some cultures even believe that it
has healing power and can cure most anything.

Because a mother's milk is with her where she goes,
she is able to feed her baby anywhere,
and some times no one else knows.

Mother's milk is one of a kind.
When the baby cries it knows.
As soon as the mother hears these sounds
her milk begins to flow.

Each and every day mothers who live in big cities
and along the country hills
are sharing their milk with their babies,
and watching with gladness as their bellies fill.

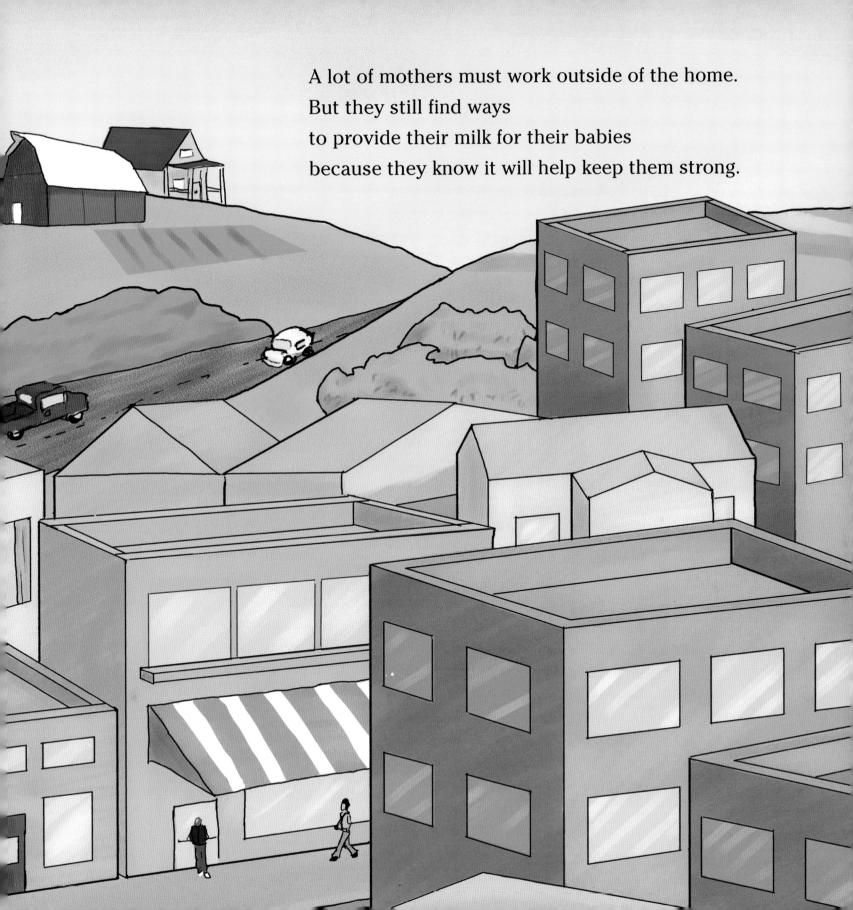

A lot of mothers must work outside of the home.
But they still find ways
to provide their milk for their babies
because they know it will help keep them strong.

Keeping our world safe and clean
is an important goal for us all to achieve.
From the air that we breathe to the fish in the sea,
it helps to keep mother's milk as safe as it can be.

Not only is mother's milk good for a new baby,
it is good for an older one too.
As long as the baby keeps eating
the mother's body knows just what to do.

Mother's milk is smart
because it knows what each and every baby needs.
Each drop is filled with many good things
so baby grows and develops with each and every feed.

So when you see a mother giving her baby her milk,
don't stare. Instead, offer a smile.
And know that she is giving the best that
she can give to her special child.